BIBLE
PROMISES
for Mom

BIBLE
PROMISES
for Mom

B&H
PUBLISHING GROUP
www.BHPublishingGroup.com
NASHVILLE, TENNESSEE

Copyright © 2014 by B&H Publishing Group

All rights reserved.

Printed in China

978-1-4336-8256-8

Printed by B&H Publishing Group, Nashville, Tennessee

Dewey Decimal Classification: 242.643

Subject Heading: CHRISTIAN LIFE \ DEVOTIONAL
LITERATURE \ MOTHERS

All Scripture quotations are taken from the Holman Christian
Standard Bible®, Copyright © 1999, 2000, 2002, 2003, 2009 by
Holman Bible Publishers. Used by permission. Holman Christian
Standard Bible®, Holman CSB®, and HCSB® are federally
registered trademarks of Holman Bible Publishers.

Quotes taken from:

The New Encyclopedia of Christian Quotations

Published by Baker Books

©2000 John Hunt Publishing Ltd.

P.O. Box 6287, Grand Rapids, MI 49516-6287

1 2 3 4 5 6 7 8 • 18 17 16 15 14

CONTENTS

INTRODUCTION

Moms may differ in the approaches they take to raising great children, but the goal is always the same. Moms want the best for their kids. They want children who can thrive in the world, make good decisions, and be thoughtful and loving human beings. They also want their children to know God.

It's a big job, but when God chose you to be a mom, He knew you had what it takes to get that job done. God's promise to you is that He will walk with you through the challenges, the joys, and the uncertainties of child-raising. He'll guide you so that you have opportunities to speak words of wisdom, or to know when to laugh, or simply when to stay quiet about something your child experiences. God will help you balance your career, your home life, and all the things that make you a wonderful woman.

With God's help, you can be sure that your children will indeed rise up and call you blessed. This book is for you, Mom! It's filled with God's promises to help you to be all you were meant to be as a mother.

God gave you a big job, but He didn't intend for you to do it all alone. Look at some of the ways He offers to share this parenting journey with you. Of course, He's always there to guide you. He's there as your loving Father, your trusted parent. God chose you for the job because He knew you'd do it well!

You are a forever blessing to your children and your family.

In His Love,
Karen Moore

CHAPTER ONE

PROMISES JUST FOR YOU

God Sees You and Cares about Your Needs

Human beings must be known to be loved:
but Divine things must be loved to be known.
~ Blaise Pascal

The day-to-day business of being a good mom is both rewarding and challenging. One sweet smile from an upturned wide-eyed little face and all is well. Some tears and tantrums and you can be worn and weary. The beauty of all of it is that when you give God just a few minutes of your time, you put your hand in His and He's there with you all through the day. He knows what a great mom you are and as your Father, He cares about all your needs. Take a look!

Don't Worry about a Thing!

Don't worry about anything, but in everything, through prayer and petition with thanksgiving, let your requests be made known to God.

And the peace of God, which surpasses every thought, will guard your hearts and your minds in Christ Jesus.
~ Philippians 4:6–7

What's for Dinner?

This is why I tell you: Don't worry about your life, what you will eat or what you will drink; or about your body, what you will wear. Isn't life more than food and the body more than clothing? Look at the birds of the sky: They don't sow or reap or gather into barns yet your heavenly Father feeds them. Aren't you worth more than they? ~ Matthew 6:25–26

But What Will I Wear?

And why do you worry about clothes? Learn how the wildflowers of the field grow: they don't labor or spin thread. Yet I tell you that not even Solomon in all his splendor was adorned like one of these!

If that's how God clothes the grass of the field, which is here today and thrown into the furnace tomorrow, won't He do much more for you—you of little faith? ~ Matthew 6:28–30

I'm Just So Tired!

Come to Me, all you who are weary and burdened, and I will give you rest. All of you, take up My yoke and learn from Me, because I am gentle and humble in heart, and you will find rest for yourselves. ~ Matthew 11:28–29

God Cares about You!

Humble yourselves, therefore, under the mighty hand of God, so that He may exalt you, casting all your care on Him, because He cares about you. ~ 1 Peter 5:6–7

You're a Gifted Mom!

Based on the gift each one has received, use it to serve others, as good managers of the varied grace of God. If anyone speaks, it should be as one who speaks God's words; if anyone serves, it should be from the strength God provides, so that God may be glorified through Jesus Christ in everything. ~ 1 Peter 4:10–11

A Blessing of Hope

Now may the God of hope fill you with all joy and peace as you believe in Him, so that you may overflow with hope by the power of the Holy Spirit. ~ Romans 15:13

God Is Near

The LORD is near all who call out to Him, all who call out to Him with integrity. ~ Psalm 145:18

Live In Him!

For in Him we live and move and exist, as even some of your own poets have said, "For we are also His offspring." ~ Acts 17:28

God Holds You Up

> Do not fear, for I am with you;
> do not be afraid, for I am your God.
> I will strengthen you; I will help you;
> I will hold on to you with My righteous
> right hand. ~ Isaiah 41:10

God Comforts Like a Mother

> As a mother comforts her son, so will I
> comfort you. ~ Isaiah 66:13

Quotes and Sayings

*God almighty is our loving Father, and God all
wisdom is our loving Mother, with the love and the
goodness of the Holy Spirit, which is all one God, one
Lord. ~ Julian of Norwich*

*I believe God is managing affairs and that He doesn't
need any advice from me. With God in charge, I believe
everything will work out for the best in the end. So what is
there to worry about? ~ Henry Ford*

God does not give us everything we want, but He does fulfill all His promises . . . leading us along the best and straightest paths to Himself. ~ Dietrich Bonhoeffer

I have experienced that the habit of taking out of the hand of our Lord every little blessing and brightness on our path, confirms us, in an especial manner, in communion with his love. ~ M. A. Schimmeleninck

Human love is capable of great things. What then must be the depth and height and intensity of divine love. Know nothing, think of nothing but Jesus Christ and him crucified. ~ Lord Shaftesbury

God is always near you and with you; leave Him not alone. ~ Brother Lawrence

The Bible gives me a deep, comforting sense that things seen are temporal, and things unseen are eternal.
~ Helen Keller

Promise and Prayer

Dear Lord, You know how much I need You each day. I need You for strength when those moments of being a mom wear me a bit thin. I need You for courage when my child is ill or in trouble in some way, and I need You for wisdom as I strive to be a loving guide and listening ear. Bless my home and my family with Your great love. Amen.

When You Need to Slow Down and Rest

All the resources of the Godhead are at our disposal! ~ Jonathan Goforth

Being a mom can keep you on the go 24/7. You can wonder if you'll ever get a full night's sleep again or if you'll ever be able to be really comfortable when the kids are at someone else's house. You may find yourself dashing to get everyone off to school, get the baby to the sitter, get to work, get home and make dinner, go to soccer practice and then to piano lessons and whatever else the kids are doing after school. You feel like it's a go, go, go life. God can run with you, but sometimes He just wants you to stop! He wants you to give all your attention to Him so He can give all His attention to you. See if that doesn't make your day a whole lot better.

Be Like a Child

> LORD, my heart is not proud; my eyes are not haughty.
> I do not get involved with things too great or too difficult for me.
> Instead, I have calmed and quieted myself like a little weaned child with its mother; I am like a little child. ~ Psalm 131:1–2

Trust In the Lord

Trust in the LORD and do what is good; dwell in the land and live securely.

Take delight in the LORD; and He will give you your heart's desires.

Commit your way to the LORD; trust in Him, and He will act, making your righteousness shine like the dawn, your justice like the noonday.

Be silent before the LORD and wait expectantly for Him. ~ Psalm 37:3–7

Find Rest

This is what the LORD says: "Stand by the roadways and look. Ask about the ancient paths: Which is the way to what is good? Then take it and find rest for yourselves." ~ Jeremiah 6:16

In Quiet Confidence

For the Lord GOD, the Holy One of Israel, has said: "You will be delivered by returning and resting; your strength will lie in quiet confidence." ~ Isaiah 30:15

Stay Calm

> Calmness puts great offenses to rest.
> ~ Ecclesiastes 10:4

God Helps Us When We Wait for Him

> I waited patiently for the LORD, and He turned to me and heard my cry for help. He brought me up from a desolate pit, out of the muddy clay, and set my feet on a rock, making my steps secure. He put a new song in my mouth, a hymn of praise to our God. ~ Psalm 40:1–3

Peaceful Sleep

> The fear of the LORD leads to life; one will sleep at night without danger.
> ~ Proverbs 19:23

Hope In the Lord

> The LORD is good to those who wait for Him, to the person who seeks Him. It is good to wait quietly for deliverance from the LORD. ~ Lamentations 3:25–26

Sit at His Feet

Let us go to His dwelling place; let us worship at His footstool. Rise up, LORD, come to Your resting place, You and Your powerful ark. May Your priests be clothed with righteousness, and may Your godly people shout for joy. ~ Psalm 132:7–9

Think Happy Thoughts

Finally brothers, whatever is true, whatever is honorable, whatever is just, whatever is pure, whatever is lovely, whatever is commendable—if there is any moral excellence and if there is any praise— dwell on these things. ~ Philippians 4:8

Quotes and Sayings

If there is righteousness in the heart, there will be beauty in the character.
If there is beauty in the character, there will be harmony in the home.
If there is harmony in the home, there will be order in the nation.
When there is order in the nation, there will be peace in the world. ~ Author Unknown

Great peace is found in little busy-ness. ~ Chaucer

And I smiled to think God's greatness flowed around our incompleteness, round our restlessness, His rest. ~ Elizabeth Barrett Browning

Let nothing good or bad upset the balance of your life. ~ Thomas à Kempis

O God, make us children of quietness, and heirs of peace. ~ Clement of Rome

Promise and Prayer

Lord, thank You for those quiet, gentle moments when we can put our cares and our activities aside, and rest in You. Thank You for those moments when all is peaceful in the house, and children are calm and at rest. Thank You that we are always under Your watchful wings. Help us to be mindful of You in all we do. Amen.

Being a Contented, Happy Woman

Contentment is a pearl of great price, and whoever procures it at the expense of ten thousand desires makes a wise and happy choice. ~ *John Balguy*

Most of us understand the beauty and value of feeling contented with what we have in life, where we are and who we are. The problem is that one or more of those things tends to get out of alignment somewhere along the way and we're left feeling discontented again. If things are going well with one child, another one will be out of sorts. If our marriage is happy, our finances are shaky. Something is always a little off. God wants us to know that though we may not be happy in all circumstances, with His help, we can be content in all situations. See what He means as you read these Scriptures.

When Things Don't Seem Good

> Though the fig tree does not bud and
> there is no fruit on the vines, though the
> olive crop fails and the fields produce no
> food, though there are no sheep in the
> pen and no cattle in the stalls, yet I will
> triumph in the Yahweh; I will rejoice in
> the God of my salvation! ~ Habakkuk
> 3:17–18

The Lord Is Like Refreshing Rain

Let us strive to know the LORD. His appearance is as sure as the dawn. He will come to us like the rain, like the spring showers that water the land.
~ Hosea 6:3

Finding Satisfaction

I will give praise in the great congregation because of You;

I will fulfill my vows before those who fear You.

The humble will eat and be satisfied; those who seek the LORD will praise Him. ~ Psalm 22:25–26

No Financial Worry

Your life should be free from the love of money. Be satisfied with what you have, for He Himself has said, I will never leave you or forsake you. ~ Hebrews 13:5

Not Falling into Temptation

But godliness with contentment is a great gain. For we brought nothing into the world, and we can take nothing out. But if we have food and clothing, we will be content with these. But those who want to be rich fall into temptation, a trap, and many foolish and harmful desires, which plunge people into ruin and destruction. For the love of money is a root of all kinds of evil, and by craving it, some have wandered away from the faith and pierced themselves with many pains. ~ 1 Timothy 6:6–10

Seek the Lord First

Those who hunger and thirst for righteousness are blessed, for they will be filled. ~ Matthew 5:6

Don't Worry about the News of the World

Do not be agitated by evildoers; do not envy those who do wrong.
    For they wither quickly like grass and wilt like tender green plants.
~ Psalm 37:1–2

How to Be Content

I have learned to be content in whatever circumstances I am. I know both how to have a little, and I know how to have a lot. In any and all circumstances I have learned the secret of being content—whether well fed or hungry, whether in abundance or in need. I am able to do all things through Him who strengthens me. ~ Philippians 4:11–13

Quotes and Sayings

The Bible belongs to those elemental things—like the sky, the wind and the sea, like the kisses of little children and tears shed beside the grave—which can never grow stale or out of date. ~ T. H. Darlow

The utmost we can hope for in this life is contentment. ~ Joseph Addison

Next to faith this is the highest art—to be content with the calling in which God has placed you. I have not learned it yet. ~ Martin Luther

It is so important not to waste what is precious by spending all one's time and emotion on fretting or complaining over what one does not have.
~ Edith Schaeffer

Being happy with God now means:
Loving as he loves,
Helping as he helps,
Giving as he gives,
Serving as he serves,
Rescuing as he rescues,
Being with him twenty-four hours,
Touching him in his distressing disguise.
~ Mother Teresa

Three grand essentials to happiness in this life are:
Something to do,
Something to love,
Something to hope for.
~ Joseph Addison

Where your pleasure is, there is your treasure; where your treasure, there your heart; where your heart, there your happiness. ~ Augustine of Hippo

Promise and Prayer

Lord, thank You for placing me right where I am. Thank You for the gifts of my family and for the work I do each day. Help me always to lean in closer to You and to be strengthened by Your presence. I am content in You and grateful for the abundance You have already given me. Amen.

Because You Always Need Security and Understanding

All, everything that I understand, I understand only because I love. ~ Tolstoy

As women, we generally process the world through our senses, heightened to even greater degrees when we become moms. We want to understand life and the things of God because the more we understand, the more secure we feel. We love with every fiber of our being and when it comes to our children, we hope to love them unconditionally, just as God loves us. Now that is a true sense of security. See here what it means to have unconditional love and understanding from God.

When We Keep the Lord in Mind

> I keep the LORD in mind always,
> Because He is at my right hand, I will not be shaken.
> Therefore my heart is glad and my spirit rejoices; my body also rests securely . . .
> You reveal the path of life to me; in Your presence is abundant joy; in Your right hand are eternal pleasures. ~ Psalm 16:8–9, 11

No Reason for Fear

The LORD is my light and my salvation—whom should I fear?
The LORD is the stronghold of my
life—of whom should I be afraid?
~ Psalm 27:1

Trusting in God

When I am afraid, I will trust in You.
In God, whose word I praise, in God
I trust; I will not fear.
What can man do to me?
~ Psalm 56:3–4

Confidence in Christ

We have this kind of confidence toward
God through Christ. It is not that we
are competent in ourselves to consider
anything as coming from ourselves, but
our competence is from God.
~ 2 Corinthians 3:4–5

Free to Be

Therefore, if the Son sets you free, you
really will be free. ~ John 8:36

Living Securely

He will stand and shepherd them in the strength of Yahweh, in the majestic name of Yahweh His God.

They will live securely, for then His greatness will extend to the ends of the earth. ~ Micah 5:4

The Lord Is My Shepherd

The LORD is my shepherd; there is nothing I lack.

He lets me lie down in green pastures;

He leads me beside quiet waters.

He renews my life; He leads me along the right paths for His name's sake.

Even when I go through the darkest valley,

I fear no danger, for You are with me;

Your rod and Your staff—they comfort me.

You prepare a table before me in the presence of my enemies;

You anoint my head with oil; my cup overflows.

Only goodness and faithful love will pursue me all the days of my life, and I will dwell in the house of the LORD as long as I live. ~ Psalm 23:1–6

God Gives Us Understanding

And we know that the Son of God has come and has given us understanding so that we may know the true One. We are in the true One—that is, in His Son Jesus Christ. He is the true God and eternal life. ~ 1 John 5:20

A Secure Future

For our momentary light affliction is producing for us an absolutely incomparable eternal weight of glory. So we do not focus on what is seen, but on what is unseen; for what is seen is temporary, but what is unseen is eternal.
~ 2 Corinthians 4:17–18

Quotes and Saying

It has pleased God that divine truths should not enter the heart through the understanding, but that understanding should come through the heart.
~ *Blaise Pascal*

Frequent combing gives the hair more luster and makes it easier to comb; a soul that frequently examines its thoughts, words, and deeds, which are its hair, doing all things for the love of God, will have lustrous hair.
~ John of the Cross

Only in growth, reform, and change, paradoxically enough, is true security to be found.
~ Anne Morrow Lindbergh

When everything we receive from him is received and prized as fruit and pledge of his covenant love, then his bounties, instead of being set up as rivals and idols to draw our heart from him, awaken us to fresh exercises of gratitude and furnish us with fresh motives of cheerful obedience every hour. ~ John Newton

Only the heart knows how to find what is precious.
~ Dostoevski

Promise and Prayer

Lord, some days it is difficult to be a woman of understanding. Being a mom is not an easy job and kids don't really come with a good "how-to" book. Thank You though that I can be secure in You, knowing that You will guide me when I need greater understanding and that You will keep me always securely by Your side. Thank You for Your infinite grace that allows me to come to You for further instruction, wisdom, and understanding. Amen.

Chapter Two

Promises for You and Your Family

As You Raise Your Children

The mind of Christ is to be learned in the family. Strength of character may be acquired at work, but beauty of character is learned at home. There the affections are trained. ~ Henry Drummond

God blessed you with a family because He knew you were exactly what they needed. As a mom, you are the heart of your home, the one who nourishes and sustains the household. You are the smile of welcome, the instant hug at the first sight of a tear, and the patient deliverer of prayers. God knew He had picked an amazing mom when He chose you to share your great love with your family. On those difficult days and on to brighter days, He's there with you. He promises!

We Are God's Children

> The Spirit Himself testifies together with our spirit that we are God's children, and if children, also heirs—heirs of God and co-heirs with Christ—seeing that we suffer with Him so that we may also be glorified with Him. For I consider that the sufferings of this present time are not worth comparing with the glory that is going to be revealed to us.
> ~ Romans 8:16–18

Peaceful and Safe

> The result of righteousness will be peace; the effect of righteousness will be quiet confidence forever. Then my people will dwell in a peaceful place, and in safe and secure dwellings. ~ Isaiah 32:17–18

Joy and Comfort

When I am filled with cares, Your comfort brings me joy. ~ Psalm 94:19

The Lord Is Good

The LORD is good, a stronghold in a day of distress;

He cares for those who take refuge in Him. ~ Nahum 1:7

His Inheritance

I pray that the perception of your mind may be enlightened so you may know what is the hope of His calling, what are the glorious riches of His inheritance among the saints, and what is the immeasurable greatness of His power to us who believe, according to the working of His vast strength. ~ Ephesians 1:18–19

Hope in God

Rather, train yourself in godliness, for, the training of the body has a limited benefit, but godliness is beneficial in every way, since it holds the promise for the present life and also for the life to come. This saying is trustworthy and deserves full acceptance. In fact, we labor and strive for this, because we have put our hope in the living God, who is the Savior of everyone, especially of those who believe. ~ 1 Timothy 4:7–10

Talk About Faith

Tell your children about it, and let your children tell their children, and their children the next generation. ~ Joel 1:3

Use Loving Discipline

Don't withhold correction from a youth. ~ Proverbs 23:13

Guide Your Children

Discipline your son, and it will bring you peace of mind and give you delight. ~ Proverbs 29:17

God Is Your Refuge

In the fear of the LORD one has strong confidence and his children have a refuge. ~ Proverbs 14:26

Quotes and Sayings

If a child lives with acceptance, he learns to love.
If a child lives with approval, he learns to like himself.
If a child lives with recognition, he learns to have a goal.
If a child lives with fairness, he learns what justice is.
If a child lives with honesty, he learns what truth is.
If a child lives with sincerity, he learns to have faith in himself and those around him.
If a child lives with love, he learns that the world is a wonderful place to live in. ~ Author Unknown

I love little children, and it is not a slight thing when they who are fresh from God, love us.
~ Charles Dickens

Children are likely to live up to what their mothers believe of them. ~ Lady Bird Johnson

A baby is God's opinion that life should go on.
~ Carl Sandburg

Before I got married, I had six theories about bringing up children; now I have six children and no theories.
~ John Wilmot, Earl of Rochester

The mother's heart is the child's school room.
~ Henry Ward Beecher

Promise and Prayer

Lord, through Your grace and love You have provided me with a beautiful family. When I'm too tired to be everything You want me to be as a mom, please strengthen me. When I forget to guide with love and kindness, please forgive me. Help me to be worthy of my home and family and Your gracious call on my life. Amen.

Continued Love and Guidance

Pride is one of the seven deadly sins;
but it cannot be the pride of a mother in her children,
for that is a compound of two cardinal virtues—
faith and hope. ~ Charles Dickens

Your love is a given because you know how to create an atmosphere of unconditional love. After all, you're a warrior when it comes to protecting your family and keeping everyone safe in your care. When things happen that feel out of your control, you know that you always have a place to go. You can always go to your Father who watches over your family with as much love as you do. He is your Source of continual love.

Children Obey Parents

Children, obey your parents as you
would the Lord, because this is right.
Honor your father and mother, which is
the first commandment with a promise,
so that it may go well with you and that
you may have a long life in the land.
~ Ephesians 6:1–3

Teaching the Young

Teach a youth about the way he should go; even when he is old he will not depart from it. ~ Proverbs 22:6

Be There for Your Children

Let Your work be seen by Your servants, and Your splendor by their children. ~ Psalm 90:16

Imitate Christ

Therefore, be imitators of God, as dearly loved children. And walk in love, as the Messiah also loved us and gave Himself for us, a sacrificial and fragrant offering to God. ~ Ephesians 5:1–2

Teach about God

Come, children, listen to me; I will teach you the fear of the LORD. Who is the man who delights in life, loving a long life to enjoy what is good? Keep your tongue from evil and your lips from deceitful speech. Turn away from evil and do what is good; seek peace and pursue it. ~ Psalm 34:11–14

Welcome Children

Whoever welcomes one little child such as this in My name welcomes Me.
~ Mark 9:37

Budget Concerns

I am not seeking what is yours, but you. For children are not obligated to save up for their parents, but parents for their children. I will most gladly spend and be spent for you. ~ 2 Corinthians 12:14–15

Words of Wisdom

I will declare wise sayings; I will speak mysteries from the past—things we have heard and known and that our fathers have passed down to us.

We must not hide them from their children, but must tell a future generation the praises of the LORD, His might, and the wonderful works He has performed.

He established a testimony in Jacob and set up a law in Israel, which He commanded our fathers to teach to their children so that a future generation— children yet to be born—might know.

They were to rise and tell their children so that they might put their confidence in God and not forget God's works, but keep His commands. ~Psalm 78:2–7

Listen to God

Command your children to carefully follow all the words of this law. For they are not meaningless words to you but they are your life. ~ Deuteronomy 32:46–47

Speak the Truth in Love

Then we will no longer be little children, tossed by the waves and blown around by every wind of teaching, by human cunning with cleverness in the techniques of deceit. But speaking the truth in love, let us grow in every way into Him who is the head—Christ. ~ Ephesians 4:14–15

Hear God's Voice

Listen and hear my voice. Pay attention and hear what I say. ~ Isaiah 28:23

Quotes and Sayings

The great academy, a mother's knee. ~ Thomas Carlyle

You have omitted to mention the greatest of my teachers—my mother. ~ Winston Churchill

The art of teaching is the art of assisting discovery. ~ Mark Van Doren

Each human mind is a galaxy of intelligences, wherein shines the light of a billion stars. ~ Timothy Ferris

Promise and Prayer

Lord, it's so wonderful to know that You are near me as I strive to be a good mom. You know what's ahead and what we need to be prepared to handle and yet You give us just one day at a time to work through. I'm grateful for Your guidance and the people You bring into my life who help sustain my efforts and my joy in being a mom. Bless my children, Lord, and Your children all around the world. Amen.

The Unique Matters
of Motherhood

Though motherhood is the most important of all the
professions—requiring more knowledge than any other
department in human affairs—there was no attention
given to preparation for this office.
~ Elizabeth Cady Stanton

Perhaps you would echo the words of Elizabeth Cady Stanton on days when somehow you don't feel prepared for the events at hand or for the challenges of motherhood. You've been called into motherhood, signed up for a lifetime task, and you may or may not feel you had adequate preparation. The beauty of this unique position is that God is aware of all you need. He knows you and His gift to you is that He'll be there, equipping you as you go to be a great mom. His promise is that He will be with you every step of the way, from toddlers to teens, to adults to grandchildren. God is by your side.

Your Strong Tower

> The name of Yahweh is a strong tower;
> the righteous run to it and are protected.
> ~ Proverbs 18:10

Your Everlasting Rock

You will keep the mind that is dependent on You in perfect peace, for it is trusting in You.

Trust in the Lord forever, because in Yah, the Lord, is an everlasting rock!
~ Isaiah 26:3–4

His Strength in Your Weakness

Therefore, I will most gladly boast all the more about my weaknesses, so that Christ's power may reside in me. . . For when I am weak, then I am strong.
~ 2 Corinthians 12:9b, 10b

When It's a Bad Day

For our momentary light affliction is producing for us an absolutely incomparable eternal weight of glory. So we do not focus on what is seen, but on what is unseen. For what is seen is temporary, but what is unseen is eternal.
~ 2 Corinthians 4:17–18

You're Doing Great! Keep Going!

So don't throw away your confidence, which has a great reward. For you need endurance, so that after you have done God's will, you may receive what was promised. ~ Hebrews 10:35–36

Children of Light

Walk as children of light—for the fruit of the light results in all goodness, righteousness, and truth—discerning what is pleasing to the Lord. ~ Ephesians 5:8–10

Moms Do Good Things

Little children, we must not love with word or speech, but with truth and action. ~ 1 John 3:18

Taking Care of Your Little Ones

See that you don't look down on one of these little ones, because I tell you that in heaven their angels continually view the face of My Father in heaven. . .

What do you think? If a man has 100 sheep, and one of them goes astray, won't he leave the 99 on the hillside, and go and search for the stray? And if he finds it, I assure you: He rejoices than over that sheep more than the 99 that did not go astray. In the same way, it is not the will of your Father in heaven that one of these little ones perish. ~ Matthew 18:10, 12–14

Rooted in Love

I pray that you, being rooted and firmly established in love, may be able to comprehend with all the saints what is the length and width, height and depth of God's love, and to know the Messiah's love that surpasses knowledge, so you may be filled with all the fullness of God. ~ Ephesians 3:17–19

Some Good Counsel

Get wisdom, get understanding; don't forget or turn away from the words of my mouth.

Don't abandon wisdom, and she will watch over you; love her, and she will guard you.

Wisdom is supreme—so get wisdom.

And whatever else you get, get understanding.

Cherish her, and she will exalt you; if you embrace her, she will honor you.

She will place a garland of grace on your head; she will give you a crown of beauty. ~ Proverbs 4:5–9

Teach Your Children

Imprint these words of mine on your hearts. . .Teach them to your children, talking about them when you sit in your house and when you walk along the road, when you lie down and when you get up. Write them on the doorposts of your house and on your gates, so that as long as the heavens are above the earth, your days and those of your children may be many. ~ Deuteronomy 11:18a, 19–21a

Be Diligent

Only be on your guard and diligently watch yourselves, so that you don't forget the things your eyes have seen and so that they don't slip from your mind as long as you live. Teach them to your children and your grandchildren.
~ Deuteronomy 4:9

Keep Growing in Love

> And I pray this: that your love will keep on growing in knowledge and every kind of discernment, so that you can approve the things that are superior and can be pure and blameless in the day of Christ, filled with the fruit of righteousness that comes through Jesus Christ to the glory and praise of God. ~ Philippians 1:9–11

You Matter to God

> This is how we know that we love God's children, when we love God and obey His commands. For this is what love for God is: to keep His commands. Now His commands are not a burden, because whatever has been born of God conquers the world. ~ 1 John 5:2–4

Quotes and Sayings

Whatever merit there is in anything that I have written is simply due to the fact that when I was a child, my mother daily read me a part of the Bible and made me learn a part of it by heart. ~ John Ruskin

Holy as heaven a mother's tender love, the love of many prayers and many tears which changes not with dim, declining years. ~ Caroline Norton

God's promises are like the stars; the darker the night, the brighter they shine. ~ David Nicholas

If you want children to keep their feet on the ground, put some responsibility on their shoulders. ~ Abigail Van Buren

A Mother Is . . .

M—Master Manager
O—Outstanding Officiator
T—Tender Teacher
H—Hopeful Heart
E—Excellent Encourager
R—Reverent and Remarkable
~ Karen Moore

Love is the fulfillment of all our works.
There is the goal; that is why we run:
we run toward it, and once we reach it,
in it we shall find rest. ~ Augustine of Hippo

Love does not dominate, it cultivates.
~ Goethe

Promise and Prayer

Thank You, Father, for loving me so much that I can better understand how to love my children in return. Thank You for teaching me and disciplining me so that I can more easily follow You and walk on the path of joy. Help me to be willing to guide, guard, and teach my children so they too can stand on their own one day and follow You, fulfilling their life work to Your glory. Amen.

Friends, Family, and Others Who Cheer Mom On!

Joy is love exalted; peace is love in repose; long-suffering is love enduring; gentleness is love in society; goodness is love in action; faith is love on the battlefield; meekness is love in school; and temperance is love in training.
~ D. L. Moody

As a mom, you're always learning new things about love. You're learning when you have to stretch to love new ideas or opportunities for your children. You're learning to love those who encourage you and help shape your thinking about parenting. You're learning what to keep and what to discard so that you can be strengthened by faith and by others and yet learn to trust what God has for you in this incredible journey. Love abounds.

Blessings

> But the one who looks intently into the perfect law of freedom and perseveres in it, and is not a forgetful hearer but one who does good work—this person will be blessed in what he does. ~ James 1:25

Family Affection and Wisdom

Love must be without hypocrisy. Detest evil; cling to what is good. Show family affection to one another with brotherly love. Outdo one another in showing honor. Do not lack diligence; be fervent in spirit; serve the Lord. Rejoice in hope; be patient in affliction; be persistent in prayer. Share with the saints in their needs; pursue hospitality. Bless those who persecute you; bless and do not curse. Rejoice with those who rejoice; weep with those who weep. Be in agreement with one another. Do not be proud; instead, associate with the humble. Do not be wise in your own estimation. Do not repay anyone evil for evil. Try to do what is honorable in everyone's eyes. If possible, on your part, live at peace with everyone. ~ Romans 12:9–18

Practice Makes Perfect

Practice these things; be committed to them, so that your progress may be evident to all. Pay close attention to your life and your teaching; persevere

in these things, for by doing this you will save both yourself and your hearers.
~ 1 Timothy 4:15–16

Love One Another

Just as I have loved you, you should also love one another. By this all people will know that you are My disciples, if you have love for one another. ~ John 13:34–35

Love God

"Which command is the most important of all?"

"This is the most important," Jesus answered:

"'Listen Israel! The Lord our God, the Lord is One. Love the Lord your God with all your heart, with all your soul, with all your mind, and with all your strength.'

"The second is: 'Love your neighbor as yourself.' There is no other command greater than these." ~ Mark 12:28–31

Carry Each Other's Burdens

Carry one another's burdens; in this way you will fulfill the law of Christ. For if anyone considers himself to be something when he is nothing, he deceives himself. But each person should examine his own work, and then he will have a reason for boasting in himself alone, and not in respect to someone else. For each person will have to carry his own load.
~ Galatians 6:2–5

Companions of Christ

For we have become companions of the Messiah if we hold firmly until the end the reality that we had at the start.
~ Hebrews 3:14

Family

But He replied to them, "My mother and My brothers are those who hear and do the word of God." ~ Luke 8:21

Keep Going

> But as for you, be strong; don't be discouraged, for your work has a reward.
> ~ 2 Chronicles 15:7

Be Confident

> Now this is the confidence we have before Him: Whenever we ask anything according to His will, He hears us. And if we know that He hears whatever we ask, we know that we have what we have asked Him for. ~ 1 John 5:14–15

Trust

> Again, I will trust in Him. And again, Here I am with the children God gave Me. ~ Hebrews 2:13

Daily Encouragement

> Encourage each other daily, while it is still called today, so that none of you is hardened by sin's deception. For we have become companions of the Messiah if we hold firmly until the end the reality that we had at the start. ~ Hebrews 3:13–14

Quotes and Sayings

*Nothing we do, however virtuous,
can be accomplished alone; therefore we
are saved by love. ~ Reinhold Niebuhr*

*Love of God is the root, love of our neighbor
the fruit of the Tree of Life. Neither can exist without
the other, but the one is cause and the other effect.
~ William Temple*

*Spread love everywhere you go: First of all in your
own house . . . let no one ever come to you without
leaving better and happier. Be the living expression of
God's kindness; kindness in your face, kindness in your
eyes, kindness in your smile, kindness in your warm
greeting. ~ Mother Teresa*

*Love is an act of endless forgiveness, a tender look
which becomes a habit. ~ Peter Ustinov*

Nothing is so strong as gentleness, nothing so gentle as real strength. ~ Francis de Sales

God is not a deceiver, that he should offer to support us, and then, when we lean upon Him, should slip away from us. ~ Augustine of Hippo

Every parent especially ought to feel, every hour of the day, that, next to making his own calling and election sure, this is the end for which he is kept alive by God, this is his task on earth. ~ R. L. Dabney

A hundred years from now it will not matter what my bank account was, the sort of house I lived in, or the kind of car I drove. But the world may be different because I was important in the life of a child.
~ Kathy Davis

Promise and Prayer

Lord, thank You for giving me the gift of being a parent. Each day, I recognize the importance of our work together to give all we can to blessing the life of a child. Thank You for watching over our plans and dreams and our health and resources. Grant that I might please You in all I do as a mom. Amen.

CHAPTER THREE

MOMS ARE PEOPLE TOO!

God's Help When You Feel Overwhelmed

*When we are weighed down by poverty, and grief makes
us sad; when bodily pain makes us restless, and exile
despondent; or when any other grievance afflicts us, if
there be good people at hand who understand the art of
rejoicing with the joyful and weeping with the sorrowful,
who know how to speak a cheerful word and uplift us,
then bitterness is mitigated, worries are alleviated and
our troubles are overcome. ~ Augustine of Hippo*

Who knows what really causes you as a mom to feel overwhelmed. It may be some of the things described in this quote, or it may be other things, but it's very likely that you just feel overloaded with all the tasks at hand. You may feel like life is totally out of control and you wonder whether God actually knows you're in great need of His help. Be assured He knows. He's not asleep in the storms of your life. He's awake and ready to help. Trust Him!

Prepare Your Mind and Heart

> Therefore, with your minds ready for action, being serious and set your hope completely on the grace to be brought to you at the revelation of Jesus Christ. As obedient children, do not be conformed to the desires of your former ignorance. But as the One who called you is holy, you also are to be holy in all your conduct; for it is written, "Be holy, because I am holy."
>
> And if you address as Father the One who judges impartially based on each one's work, you are to conduct yourselves in fear during the time of your temporary residence.
>
> For all flesh is like grass, and all its glory like a flower of the grass. The grass withers, and the flower falls, but

the word of the Lord endures forever.
And this is the word that was preached
as the gospel to you. ~ 1 Peter 1:13–17,
24–25

Prayer for Strength

God, hear my cry; pay attention to my
prayer.

I call to You from the ends of the
earth when my heart is without strength.

Lead me to a rock that is high above
me, for You have been a refuge for me, a
strong tower in the face of the enemy.
~ Psalm 61:1–3

God Hears Your Cry

I cry aloud to the LORD; I plead aloud to
the LORD for mercy. I pour out my complaint before Him; I reveal my trouble to
Him. Although my spirit is weak within
me, You know my way. ~ Psalm 142:1–3

Your Portion Forever

You guide me with Your counsel, and
afterward You will take me up in glory.
Who do I have in heaven but You? And

I desire nothing on earth but You. My
flesh and my heart may fail, but God is
the strength of my heart, my portion
forever. ~ Psalm 73:24–26

Renewing Your Strength

I love You, Lord, my strength. The Lord
is my rock, my fortress, and my deliverer,
my God, my mountain where I seek
refuge, my shield and the horn of my
salvation, my stronghold. ~ Psalm 18:1–2

The Wonder of God

Has God forgotten to be gracious?
Has He in anger withheld His compassion? . . . I will remember the Lord's
works; yes, I will remember Your ancient
wonders. I will reflect on all You have
done and meditate on Your actions. . . .
You are the God who works wonders;
You revealed Your strength among the
people. ~ Psalm 77:9, 11–12, 14

God Is With You

God, You are my God; I eagerly seek
You. I thirst for You; my body faints for

You in a land that is dry, desolate, and without water. So I gaze on You in the sanctuary to see Your strength and Your glory. My lips will glorify You because Your faithful love is better than life. So I will praise You as long as I live; at Your name, I will lift up my hands. You satisfy me as with rich food; my mouth will praise You with joyful lips. ~ Psalm 63:1–5

Your Guiding Light

LORD, You are my lamp; the LORD illuminates my darkness. With You I can attack a barrier, and with my God I can leap a wall . . . For who is God besides the LORD? And who is a rock? Only our God? God is my strong refuge; He makes my way perfect. ~ 2 Samuel 22:29–30, 32–33

Your Protective Shield

Finally, be strengthened by the Lord and by His vast strength. Put on the full armor of God so that you can stand against the tactics of the Devil.

For our battle is not against flesh and blood, but against the rulers, against the authorities, against the world powers of this darkness, against the spiritual forces of evil in the heavens.

This is why you must take up the full armor of God, so that you may be able to resist in the evil day, and having prepared everything, to take your stand.

In every situation take the shield of faith, and with it you will be able to extinguish the flaming arrows of the evil one. Take the helmet of salvation, and the sword of the Spirit, which is God's word. ~ Ephesians 6:10–13, 16–17

God Knows Your Name

Do not fear, for I have redeemed you; I have called you by your name; you are Mine. I will be with you when you pass through the waters, and when you pass through the rivers, they will not over-whelm you. You will not be scorched when you walk through the fire, and the flame will not burn you. For I Yahweh your God, the Holy One of Israel, and your Savior. ~ Isaiah 43:1–3

Walk with God

When you walk, your steps will not be hindered; when you run, you will not stumble. ~ Proverbs 4:12

Quotes and Sayings

Let us remember that the only way to keep our life peaceful and happy is to keep the heart at rest, for come poverty, come wealth, come honor, come shame, come plenty, or come scarcity, if the heart be quiet, there will be happiness anywhere. But whatever the sunshine and the brightness, if the heart be troubled, the whole life must be troubled too. ~ C. H. Spurgeon

The Holy Spirit is no skeptic. He has written neither doubt nor mere opinion into our hearts, but rather solid assurances, which are more sure and solid than all experience and even life itself. ~ Martin Luther

A pure, simple, and steadfast spirit is not distracted by the number of things to be done, because it performs them all to the honor of God, and endeavors to be at rest from self-seeking. ~ Thomas à Kempis

Knowing that I am not the one in control gives great encouragement. Knowing the One who is in control is everything. ~ Alexander Michael

Promise and Prayer

Lord, thank You for being in control of my life and of all the things on my to-do list. Help me to make You a priority in all that I do so I might rest in You even when I'm busy and feeling overwhelmed. Bless my home and my family in Your grace and mercy and grant me a peaceful heart to do the work You've called me to do. Amen.

Stomping Out the Negatives . . . Those Frustrated Feelings!

Expect people to be better than they are; it helps them to become better. But don't be disappointed when they are not; it helps them to keep trying. ~ Merry Browne

Sometimes being a mom brings moments of frustration. You might become frustrated that the kids don't pick up their clothes, even though you'd asked them to do so a hundred times. You might feel frustrated that your family doesn't seem to recognize all the little things you do to keep the household running smoothly. You might simply feel disappointed that so many things you hoped for when you became a mom don't seem to be happening. Today's reality needs to change. When you're frustrated with your home, your life, or yourself, see how God can help.

Depend on God

Why do you assert: "My way is hidden from the LORD, and my claim is ignored by my God?"

Do you not know? Have you not heard? Yahweh is the everlasting God, the Creator of the whole earth. He never grows faint or weary; there is no limit to His understanding. He gives strength to

the weary and strengthens the power-
less. ~ Isaiah 40:27–29

Is this a Test?

Dear friends, don't be surprised when
the fiery ordeal comes among you to
test you as if something unusual were
happening to you. Instead, rejoice as you
share in the sufferings of the Messiah, so
that you may also rejoice with great joy
at the revelation of His glory.
~ 1 Peter 4:12–13

Clear Your Mind

Do not be conformed to this age, but
be transformed by the renewing of your
mind, so that you may discern what is
the good, pleasing, and perfect will of
God. ~ Romans 12:2

Following Jesus

If anyone wants to come with Me, he
must deny himself, take up his cross
daily, and follow Me. For whoever wants
to save his life will lose it, but whoever
loses his life because of Me will save it.
~ Luke 9:23–24

God Is Your Protection

I lift my eyes toward the mountains.
Where will my help come from? My
help comes from the LORD, the Maker
of heaven and earth. He will not allow
your foot to slip; your Protector will not
slumber. Indeed, the Protector of Israel
does not slumber or sleep. The LORD
protects you; the LORD is a shelter right
by your side. The sun will not strike you
by day, or the moon by night. The LORD
will protect you from all harm; He will
protect your life. The LORD will protect
your coming and going both now and
forever. ~ Psalm 121:1–8

Keeping Christ in Your Heart

If our conscience doesn't condemn us,
we have confidence before God, and
can receive whatever we ask from Him
because we keep His commands and do
what is pleasing in His sight.

Now this is His command: that we
believe in the name of His Son Jesus
Christ, and love one another as He commanded us. The one who keeps His commands remains in Him, and He in him.
And the way we know that He remains in

us is from the Spirit He has given us.
~ 1 John 3:21–24

Setting Priorities

So don't worry, saying, "What will we eat?" or "What will we drink?" or "What will we wear?" For the idolaters eagerly seek all these things, and your heavenly Father knows that you need them. But seek first the kingdom of God and His righteousness, and all things will be provided for you. ~ Matthew 6:31–33

A Reward Awaits

Charm is deceptive and beauty is fleeting, but a woman who fears the LORD will be praised. Give her the reward of her labor, and let her works praise her at the city gates. ~ Proverbs 31:30–31

An Effort to Be Wise

Indeed, I took all this to heart and explained it all: the righteous, the wise, and their works are in God's hands. People don't know whether to expect love or hate. Everything lies ahead of them. ~ Ecclesiastes 9:1

Keep Your Eye on the Prize

> Whatever you do, do it enthusiastically, as something for the Lord and not for men, knowing that you will receive the reward of an inheritance from the Lord. You serve the Lord Christ. ~ Colossians 3:23–24

Quotes and Sayings

Watch your thoughts; they become words.
Watch your words; they become actions.
Watch your actions; they become habits.
Watch your habits; they become character.
Watch your character; for it becomes your destiny!
~ Author Unknown

A Christian is a person who thinks in believing and believes in thinking. ~ Augustine

Change your thoughts and you change your world.
~ Norman Vincent Peale

We are to be children in heart, not in understanding.
~ Thomas Aquinas

We must accept finite disappointment, but we must never lose infinite hope. ~ Martin Luther King

Most of the important things in the world have been accomplished by people who have kept on trying when there seemed to be no hope at all. ~ Dale Carnegie

I simply can't build my hopes on a foundation of confusion, misery and death . . . I think . . . peace and tranquility will return again. ~ Anne Frank

Promise and Prayer

Lord, it helps so much to know that You are always near, that Your steadfast love for me is not based on my feelings of success or failure. It is not always easy to manage my role as a mom, with expectations from my job or my community or even my friends. Sometimes, it just makes me weary and causes me a lot of frustration. Please help me to stay strong and to become all that You would have me be. In Jesus' name, I ask. Amen.

Some Emotions Don't Serve Me Well!

A wise old owl sat on an oak,
The more he saw the less he spoke;
The less he spoke the more he heard:
Why aren't we like that wise old bird?
~ Edward Hersey Richards

Some emotions don't seem to serve us very well. You know the ones: anger, bitterness, regret, jealousy, and others. These emotions are the reminders of how far we have to go to become more of what God knows we can be. We are worthy of great things and we have beautiful hearts. God knows that about us and wants us to see the gifts that come with self-control and hope. Reflect on those things that may apply to your own life, at least now and again. God is ready to help.

Sense of Loss

You have distanced loved one and neighbor from me; darkness is my only friend.
~Psalm 88:18

Try Again

Do not rejoice over me, my enemy!
Though I have fallen, I will stand up.

Though I sit in darkness, the LORD will
be my light. ~ Micah 7:8

Walking in God's Spirit

If our conscience doesn't condemn us,
we have confidence before God and
can receive whatever we ask from Him
because we keep His commands and do
what is pleasing in His sight.

Now this is His command: that we
believe in the name of His Son Jesus
Christ, and love one another as He commanded us. The one who keeps His commands remains in Him, and He in him.
And the way we know that He remains in
us is from the Spirit He has given us.
~1 John 3:21–24

An Example of God's Help and Love

The LORD is gracious and righteous; our
God is compassionate. The LORD guards
the inexperienced; I was helpless, and He
saved me. Return to your rest, my soul,
for the LORD has been good to you. For
You, LORD, rescued me from death, my
eyes from tears, my feet from stumbling.
I will walk before the LORD in the land of

the living. I believed, even when I said,
"I am severely afflicted." In my alarm
I said, "Everyone is a liar." How can
I repay the Lord all the good He has
done for me? I will take the cup of salvation and call on the name of Yahweh.
I will fulfill my vows to the Lord in
the presence of all His people. ~ Psalm
116:5–14

Your Spirit of Power and Love

For God has not given us a spirit of
fearfulness, but one of power, love, and
sound judgment. ~ 2 Timothy 1:7

Those Hidden Faults

Who perceives his unintentional sins?
Cleanse me from my hidden faults.
Moreover, keep Your servant from
willful sins; do not let them rule over
me. . . May the words of my mouth
and the meditation of my heart be
acceptable to You, Lord, my rock and
my Redeemer. ~ Psalm 19:12–13a, 14

Don't Get Agitated

Refrain from anger and give up your rage; do not be agitated—it can only bring harm. ~ Psalm 37:8

God's Will for You

For it is God's will that you silence the ignorance of foolish people be doing good. ~ 1 Peter 2:15

Be Kind

A gentle answer turns away anger, but a harsh word stirs up wrath. ~ Proverbs 15:1

Think About Your Words

Understand this: everyone must be quick to hear, slow to speak, and slow to anger, for man's anger does not accomplish God's righteousness. ~ James 1:19–20

Be a Good Neighbor

Each one of us must please his neighbor for his good, in order to build him up. For even the Messiah did not please Himself. On the contrary, as it is written,

"The insults of those who insult You have fallen on Me." ~ Romans 15:2–3

Beautiful You

Therefore, God's chosen ones, holy and loved, put on heartfelt compassion, kindness, humility, gentleness, and patience, accepting one another and forgiving one another if anyone has a complaint against another. Just as the Lord has forgiven you, so also you must forgive.

Above all, put on love—the perfect bond of unity. And let the peace of the Messiah, to which you were also called in one body, control your hearts. Be thankful.

Let the message about the Messiah dwell richly among you, teaching and admonishing one another in all wisdom, and singing psalms, hymns, and spiritual songs, with gratitude in your hearts to God. ~ Colossians 3:12–16

A Helpful Hint

And whatever you do, in word or in deed, do everything in the name of the Lord Jesus, giving thanks to God the Father through Him. ~ Colossians 3:17

That Still Golden Rule

I say to you who listen: Love your enemies, do good to those who hate you, bless those who curse you, pray for those who mistreat you.

If anyone hits you on the cheek, offer the other also. And if anyone takes away your coat, don't hold back your shirt either. Give to everyone who asks you, and from one who takes away your things, don't ask for them back. Just as you want others to do for you, do the same for them.

If you love those who love you, what credit is that to you? Even sinners love those who love them. If you do what is good to those who are good to you, what credit is that to you? Even sinners do that . . . But love your enemies, do what is good, and lend, expecting nothing in return. Then your reward will be great.
~ Luke 6:27–33, 35

Blessed Emotions

Now finally, all of you should be like-minded and sympathetic, should love believers, and be compassionate and humble, not paying back evil for evil or insult for insult but, on the contrary, giving a blessing, since you were called for this, so that you can inherit a blessing. ~ 1 Peter 3:8–9

Compassionate You

No foul language is to come from your mouth, but only what is good for building up someone in need, so that it gives grace to those who hear. All bitterness, anger and wrath, shouting and slander must be removed from you, along with all malice. And be kind and compassionate to one another, forgiving one another, just as God also forgave you in Christ. ~ Ephesians 4:29, 31–32

Be In Agreement with Others

Now may the God who gives endurance and encouragement allow you to live in harmony with one another, according to the command of Christ Jesus, so that you may glorify the God and Father of our Lord Jesus Christ with a united mind and voice. ~ Romans 15:5–6

Quotes and Sayings

Let go of your attachment to being right, and suddenly your mind is more open. You're able to benefit from the unique viewpoints of others, without being crippled by your own judgment. ~ Ralph Marston

Who is so wise as to have a perfect knowledge of all things? Therefore trust not too much to your own opinion, but be ready also to hear the opinion of others. ~ Thomas à Kempis

What lies beyond us and what lies before us are tiny matters compared to what lies within us. ~ Emerson

Small kindnesses, small courtesies, small considerations, habitually practiced in our social interactions, give a greater charm to the character than the display of great talents and accomplishments. ~ Mary Ann Kelty

Helping others, that's the main thing. The only way for us to help ourselves is to help others and to listen to each other's stories. ~ Eli Wiesel

Promise and Prayer

Lord, forgive me when I let my emotions control my actions. Help me to know when to speak in kindness and love, when to stand up for myself or my children in positive and clear ways, and how I can best honor You in all circumstances and situations. Bless me with a more compassionate and giving spirit and help me to see You in each person I meet. I pray You'll lift me from those emotions that do not serve me, my family, or You very well. Amen.

Chapter Four

God's Promises for Your Life

The Beautiful Benefits of Being a Prayerful Mom

Love to pray. Feel often during the day the need for prayer, and take trouble to pray. Prayer enlarges the heart until it is capable of containing God's gift of Himself. Ask and seek and your heart will grow big enough to receive Him. ~ Mother Teresa

Prayer is like love. You can't awake to the day without sensing your need for it and your desire to draw close to the One who knows you by name. Whatever you're going through, He is near. You can put your hopes and concerns for your children before Him and He will be a compassionate listener and seek your good in all that you ask. God devised prayer as a way for us to know Him better. You already know that the best relationships are the ones where you can be yourself and talk about anything. God wants you to be in the best relationship possible with Him. Take time to pray today.

Morning Prayer

> Let me experience Your faithful love in the morning, for I trust in You. Reveal to me the way I should go because I long for You. Rescue me from my enemies, Lord; I come to You for protection. Teach me to do Your will, for You are my God. May Your gracious Spirit lead me on level ground. ~ Psalm 143:8–10

God Hears You

> Now this is the confidence we have before Him: Whenever we ask anything according to His will, He hears us. And if we know that He hears whatever we ask, we know that we have what we have asked Him for. ~ 1 John 5:14–15

Don't Stop Asking

Keep asking, and it will be given to you. Keep searching, and you will find. Keep knocking, and the door will be opened to you. ~ Matthew 7:7

His Mercy and Grace

Therefore let us approach the throne of grace with boldness, so that we may receive mercy and find grace to help us at the proper time. ~ Hebrews 4:16

Thanks Be to God

We give thanks to You, God; we give thanks to You, for Your name is near. People tell about Your wonderful works. ~ Psalm 75:1

The Lord Is Near You

The Lord is near all who call out to Him, all who call out to Him with integrity. He fulfills the desires of those who fear Him; He hears their cry for help and saves them. ~ Psalm 145:18–19

God's Promises

Come to terms with God and be at peace; in this way good will come to you. Receive instruction from His mouth, and place His sayings in your heart. . . .

You will pray to Him, and He will hear you, and you will fulfill your vows.

When you make a decision, it will be carried out, and light will shine on your ways. ~ Job 22: 21–22, 27–28

Ask God for Wisdom

Now if any of you lacks wisdom, he should ask God, who gives to all generously and without criticizing, and it will be given to him. ~ James 1:5

Even Before You Ask

Even before they call, I will answer; while they are still speaking, I will hear. ~ Isaiah 65:24

God's Blessings for You

LORD my God, You have done many
things—Your wonderful works and Your
plans for us; none can compare with You.
If I were to report and speak of them,
they are more than can be told. ~ Psalm
40:5

Pray with a Friend

Again, I assure you: If two of you on
earth agree about any matter that you
pray for, it will be done for you by My
Father in heaven. For where two or three
are gathered together in My name, I am
there among them. ~ Matthew 18:19–20

Prayer and Peace

Don't worry about anything, but in
everything, through prayer and petition
with thanksgiving, let your requests be
made known to God. And the peace of
God, which surpasses every thought, will
guard your hearts and minds in Christ
Jesus. ~ Philippians 4:6–7

Quotes and Sayings

The pure prayer that ascends from a faithful heart will be like incense rising from a hallowed altar.
~ Augustine of Hippo

Prayer is not conquering God's reluctance, but taking hold of God's willingness. ~ Phillips Brooks

Prayer is a sincere, sensible, affectionate pouring out of the soul to God, through Christ in the strength and assistance of the Spirit, for such things as God has promised. ~ John Bunyan

One single grateful thought raised to heaven is the most perfect prayer. ~ G. E. Lessing

I have so much to do that I spend several hours in prayer before I am able to do it. ~ Martin Luther

*God always has an open ear and a ready hand,
if you have an open and ready heart.
Take your groanings and your sighs to God
and he will answer you. ~ C. H. Spurgeon*

*The life of prayer is just love to God, and the custom of
being ever with Him. ~ St. Teresa of Avila*

Promise and Prayer

Lord, thank You for Your willingness to hear my prayers. You know that I don't always know what to say, but it helps me to know that You can hear my heart even when my words aren't exactly right. Thank You for watching over my family and each person who means so much to me in my life. It's so comforting to know You are always near. Amen.

You Teach Me So Much about Love!

Let us make God the beginning and the end of our love,
for he is the fountain from which all good things flow
and into him alone they flow back. Let him therefore be
the beginning of our love. ~ Richard Rolle

As a mom and as a woman, you're always learning something new about love. No doubt, you'll be a student of love all your life, for love is always beckoning you to desire more of it, to stretch and grow and understand how great and vast and endless it truly is. God designed you to love, and actually created you from His love. Draw near to His loving heart every possible moment. He is always near to you.

God's Love for You

Look at how great a love the Father has given us that we should be called God's children. And we are! . . . Dear friends, we are God's children now, and what we will be has not yet been revealed. We know that when He appears, we will be like Him, because we will see Him as He is. And everyone who has this hope in Him purifies himself just as He is pure.
~ 1 John 3:1a, 2–3

Christ's Love for You

Rarely will someone die for a just person—though for a good person perhaps someone might even dare to die. But God proves His own love for us in that while we were still sinners, Christ died for us! ~ Romans 5:7–8

Love and Friends

No one has greater love than this, that someone would lay down his life for his friends. ~ John 15:13

God Is Love

And we have come to know and to believe the love that God has for us. God is love and the one who remains in love remains in God, and God remains in him.

In this, love is perfected with us so that we may have confidence in the day of judgment; for we are as He is in this world. There is no fear in love; instead, perfect love drives out fear, because fear involves punishment. So the one who fears has not reached perfection in love. We love because He first loved us. ~ 1 John 4:16–19

What Love Is

Love consists in this: not that we loved God, but that He loved us and sent His Son to be the propitiation for our sins. Dear friends, if God loved us in this way, we also must love one another.

No one has ever seen God. If we love one another, God remains in us and His love is perfected in us. ~ 1 John 4:10–12

Your Value

Aren't two sparrows sold for a penny? Yet not one of them falls to the ground without your Father's consent. But even the hairs of your head have all been counted. So don't be afraid therefore; you are worth more than many sparrows. ~ Matthew 10:29–31

God Chose You

You did not choose Me, but I chose you. I appointed you that you should go out and produce fruit, and that your fruit should remain, so that whatever you ask the Father in My name, He will give you. ~ John 15:16

His Love Sets Us Free

To Him who loves us and has set us free
from our sins by His blood, and made
us a kingdom, priests to His God and
Father—the glory and dominion are His
forever and ever. ~ Revelation 1:5–6

Nothing Separates Us from God

Who can separate us from the love of
Christ? Can affliction or anguish or per-
secution or famine or nakedness or danger or sword? . . . No, in all these things
we are more than victorious through Him
who loved us. For I am persuaded that not
even death or life, angels or rulers, things
present or things to come, hostile powers, height or depth, or any other created
thing will have the power to separate us
from the love of God that is in Christ
Jesus our Lord! ~ Romans 8:35, 37–39

Living in Christ

I have been crucified with Christ and I no
longer live, but Christ lives in me. The
life I now live in the body, I live by faith in
the Son of God, who loved me and gave
Himself for me. ~ Galatians 2:19–20

Living In Him

But whoever keeps His word, truly in him the love of God is perfected. This is how we know we are in Him: The one who says he remains in Him should walk just as He walked. ~ 1 John 2:5–6

A Loving Wish

To those who are the called, loved by God the Father and kept by Jesus Christ. May mercy, peace, and love be multiplied to you. ~ Jude 1–2

Quotes and Sayings

A loving heart is the truest wisdom.
~ Charles Dickens

The greatest gift is a portion of thyself.
~ Emerson

Love is an act of faith, and whoever is of little faith is also of little love. ~ Erich Fromm

You're one of the best examples of love your child will ever know. ~ Karen Moore

It is better to build strong children than to try to repair adults. ~ Author Unknown

Promise and Prayer

Dear Lord, Thank You for teaching me about Your love and for giving me the example of so many people who have taught me what love is and how to share it. You teach us to love unconditionally and You help us grow up to an understanding of all that love can be. Thank You for Your love and for each child in this world. Amen.

Your Promises Unfold with Praise and Gratitude

When we wake up each morning, if praise of the Risen Christ were to fill our hearts . . . then in the monotony of daily life, an inner surge of vitality would reveal our hidden longing. ~ Brother Roger

When you're raising children, life is full and yet at times, it can feel like the focus on your children is so strong that you're not able to create the balance between being a mom and being a woman with many other talents and interests. Whatever your sense of the balance may be, the opportunity to experience real joy and fullness in every aspect of life comes from a heart of gratitude. Praise God for all that He has done to bless your life. He'll help you keep a joyful balance.

Worship God

> Come, let us worship and bow down;
> let us kneel before the LORD our Maker.
> For He is our God, and we are the
> people of His pasture, the sheep under
> His care. ~ Psalm 95:6–7

God Knew You from Birth

For You are my hope, Lord God, my
confidence from my youth. I have leaned
on You from birth; You took me from
my mother's womb. My praise is always
about You. ~ Psalm 71:5–6

God Holds Your Future

Lord, You are my portion and my cup of
blessing; You hold my future.

The boundary lines have fallen for
me in pleasant places; indeed, I have a
beautiful inheritance.

I will praise the Lord who coun-
sels me—even at night my conscience
instructs me. I keep the Lord in mind
always. Because He is at my right hand, I
will not be shaken. ~ Psalm 16:5–8

Blessed Be the Lord

Praise the God and Father of our Lord
Jesus Christ. According to His great
mercy, He has given us a new birth into
a living hope through the resurrection of
Jesus Christ from the dead and into an
inheritance that is imperishable, uncor-
rupted, and unfading, kept in heaven for

you. You are being protected by God's power through faith for a salvation that is ready to be revealed in the last time. You rejoice in this, though now for a short time you have had to struggle in various trials so that the genuineness of your faith—more valuable than gold, which perishes though refined by fire—may result in praise, glory, and honor at the revelation of Jesus Christ. ~ 1 Peter 1:3–7

Sing to God

How good it is to sing to our God, for praise is pleasant and lovely. ~ Psalm 147:1

Nighttime Praise

When I think of You as I lie on my bed, I meditate on You during the night watches because You are my helper; I will rejoice in the shadow of Your wings. I follow close to You; Your right hand holds on to me. ~ Psalm 63:6–8

Give Thanks

Let them give thanks to the LORD for His faithful love and His wonderful works for all humanity. For He has satisfied the thirsty and filled the hungry with good things. ~ Psalm 107:8–9

Continue in Praise

Praise the God and Father of our Lord Jesus Christ, who has blessed us in Christ with every spiritual blessing in the heavens. For He chose us in Him, before the foundation of the world, to be holy and blameless in His sight. In love He predestined us to be adopted through Jesus Christ for Himself, according to His favor and will, to the praise of His glorious grace that He favored us with in the Beloved. We have redemption in Him through His blood, the forgiveness of our trespasses, according to the riches of His grace that He lavished on us with all wisdom and understanding.
~ Ephesians 1:3–8

You Were Chosen

But you are a chosen race, a royal priest-hood, a holy nation, a people for His possession, so that you may proclaim the praises of the One who called you out of darkness into His marvelous light. Once you were not a people, but now you are God's people; you had not received mercy, but now you have received mercy. ~ 1 Peter 2:9–10

Give Thanks in Everything

Give thanks in everything, for this is God's will for you in Christ Jesus. ~ 1 Thessalonians 5:18

Quotes and Sayings

If I were a nightingale, I would sing like a nightingale; if a swan, like a swan. But since I am a rational creature my role is to praise God. ~ Epictetus

This day and your life are God's gift to you: so give thanks and be joyful always! ~ Jim Beggs

A thankful heart is not only the greatest virtue, but the parent of all other virtues. ~ Cicero

A simple grateful thought raised to heaven is the most perfect prayer. ~ Gotthold Lessing

A life in thankfulness releases the glory of God. ~ Bengt Sundberg

Let us be grateful to people who make us happy—they are the charming gardeners who make our souls blossom. ~ Marcel Proust

Promise and Prayer

Lord, my heart is truly filled with gratitude for all You have done in my life. You have blessed my home and granted me the gift of motherhood. You have offered me opportunities to grow in under-standing of all it means to love others and to love You. I do not have enough words to give You true thanks and praise, but I am grateful to You beyond measure. Amen.

God's Promises for an Abundant Life

How far you go in life depends on your being tender with the young, compassionate with the aged, sympathetic with the striving, and tolerant of the weak and strong; because, someday in your life, you will have been all of these. ~ George Washington Carver

You've probably heard the saying that refers to your life as being God's gift to you and that what you make of that life is your gift back to God. Well, the same holds true for you as a mom. Your children are God's gift to you and how you help them grow and succeed in life is your gift back to God as well. God will help you in that process so that you can make each day count and be the kind of mom He knew you would be. Look to Him for all you need because He's always there. That's a promise!

Jesus Loves Your Child

> Then children were brought to Him so He might put His hands on them and pray. But the disciples rebuked them. Then Jesus said, "Leave the children alone, and don't try to keep them from coming to Me, because the kingdom of heaven is made up of people like this." ~ Matthew 19:13–14

Joy in Parenting

Let your father and mother have joy,
and let her who gave birth to you
rejoice. ~ Proverbs 23:25

A Happy Home

Even a sparrow finds a home, and a
swallow, a nest for herself where she
places her young—near Your altars,
Lord of Hosts, my King and my God.
How happy are those who reside in
your house, who praise You continually.
Happy are the people whose strength is
in You, whose hearts are set on pilgrim-
age. ~ Psalm 84:3–5

God's Blessing

You will eat there in the presence of the
Lord you God and rejoice with your
household in everything you do, because
the Lord you God has blessed you.
~ Deuteronomy 12:7

Children Are a Reward

Sons are indeed a heritage from the
Lord, children, a reward. ~ Psalm 127:3

God's Gift

He gives the childless woman a household, making her the joyful mother of children. ~ Psalm 113:9

Walk in Truth

I have no greater joy than this: to hear that my children are walking in the truth. ~ 3 John 4

A Life of Blessing

I have been young and now I am old, yet I have not seen the righteous abandoned or his children begging bread. He is always generous, always lending, and his children are a blessing. ~ Psalm 37:25–26

Welcome Child

And whoever welcomes one child like this in My name welcomes Me. ~ Matthew 18:5

A Life of Obedience and Joy

If you faithfully obey the LORD your God and are careful to follow all His

commands I am giving you today, the LORD your God will put you far above all the nations of the earth. All these blessings will come upon you and over-take you, because you obey the LORD your God: You will be blessed in the city and blessed in the country. Your descendants will be blessed, and your land's produce, and the offspring of your livestock, including the young of your herds and the newborn of your flocks. Your basket and kneading bowl will be blessed. You will be blessed when you come in and blessed when you go out.
~ Deuteronomy 28:1–6

God Knows You

I will praise You because I have been remarkably and wonderfully made. Your works are wonderful, and I know this very well. My bones were not hidden from You when I was made in secret, when I was formed in the depths of the earth. Your eyes saw me when I was formless; all my days were written in Your book and planned before a single one of them began. God, how difficult Your thoughts are for me to compre-hend; how vast their sum is! If I counted them, they would outnumber the grains of sand; when I wake up, I am still with You. ~ Psalm 139:14–18

A Blessing

May the LORD add to your numbers, both yours and your children's. May you be blessed by the LORD, the Maker of heaven and earth. The heavens are the LORD's, but the earth He has given to the human race. ~ Psalm 115:14–16

God Watches Over You

May Yahweh bless you and protect you; may Yahweh make His face shine on you and be gracious to you; may Yahweh look with favor on you and give you peace. ~ Numbers 6:24–26

Happiness Comes from God

Happy are the people with such blessings. Happy are the people whose GOD is Yahweh. ~ Psalm 144:15

A Joyful Heart

A joyful heart makes a face cheerful, but
a sad heart produces a broken spirit.
~ Proverbs 15:13

Peace

A tranquil heart is life to the body.
~ Proverbs 14:30

Quotes and Sayings

Take time to think: it is the course of power.
Take time to play: it is the secret to perpetual youth.
Take time to read: it is the fountain of wisdom.
Take time to laugh: it is the music of the soul.
Take time to give: it is too short a day to be selfish.
~ Author Unknown

Your children are a mirror which reflects back on you
the kind of image you cast. ~ Fulton Sheen

Train your child in the way in which you know you should have gone yourself. ~ C. H. Spurgeon

It's always been my feeling that God lends you your children until they are about eighteen years old. If you haven't made your points with them by then, it's too late. ~ Betty Ford

Children miss nothing in sizing up their parents. If you are only half convinced of your beliefs, they will quickly discern that fact. ~ James Dobson

Enjoy one another and take the time to enjoy family life together. Quality time is no substitute for quantity time. Quantity time is quality time. ~ Billy Graham

Promise and Prayer

Lord, always and in all ways, I am thankful to You for my life and for giving me the chance to be a mother. You know me better than I know myself and so I trust You to guide me in the ways I serve them as an example and ask you to give me wisdom to do a good job. Bless my children in all areas of life and help them to always seek You in the things they do from now and forever. Amen.

Today, Tomorrow, and Always

Be thou a bright flame before me,
Be thou a guiding star above me,
Be thou a smooth path below me,
Be thou a kindly shepherd behind me,
Today—tonight—and forever. ~ Columba of Iona

As a mom, you might wish you could always be right where your children need you to be so that you can protect them or guide them or simply let them know they are not alone. That same desire is the one God has when He wishes to be near you, to walk beside you wherever you go. God wants to protect your life and your spirit, your heart and your mind. As this ancient prayer suggests, the desire of the heart of any believer is for God to be a faithful and continual presence. You can trust that God is with you right now.

God promises to be beside you, to go before you, and to be wherever you are because nothing can separate you from Him and His incredible love. As you go about your life today and in the days ahead, embrace Him and thank Him for being a beacon of hope and light and a faithful guide for each day. Let God in to be part of everything you are now and everything you hope to be in the days to come.

The Reason to Rejoice

The LORD reigns! Let the earth rejoice; let the many coasts and islands be glad. Clouds and thick darkness surround Him; righteousness and justice are the foundation of His throne. Fire goes before Him and burns up His foes on every side. His lightning lights up the world; the earth sees and trembles.
~ Psalm 97:1–4

God Is There to Keep You Strong

For the eyes of Yahweh roam throughout the earth to show Himself strong for those whose hearts are completely His.
~ 2 Chronicles 16:9

The Lord Is Near!

The LORD is near all who call out to Him, all who call out to Him with integrity. He fulfills the desires of those who fear Him; He hears their cry for help and saves them. The LORD guards all those who love Him. ~ Psalm 145:18–20

God Fills Every Hidden Place

"Am I a God who is only near"—this is the Lord's declaration—"and not a God who is far away? Can a man hide himself in secret places where I cannot see him?"—the Lord's declaration. "Do I not fill the heavens and the earth?"—the Lord's declaration. ~ Jeremiah 23:23–24

Where There Are Two

For where two or three are gathered together in My name, I am there among them. ~ Matthew 18:20

We Exist through Him

For in Him we live and move and exist, as even some of your own poets have said, "For we are also His offspring." ~ Acts 17:28

Pray When You Feel God Is Near You

The Lord is near. Don't worry about anything, but in everything through prayer and petition with thanksgiving, let your requests be made known to God. And the peace of God, which surpasses

every thought, will guard your hearts
and your minds in Christ Jesus.
~ Philippians 4:5–7

What Can Separate Us from God?

Who can separate us from the love of
Christ? Can affliction or anguish or per-
secution or famine or nakedness or danger or sword? As it is written: Because
of You we are being put to death all
day long; we are counted as sheep to be
slaughtered. No, in all these things we
are more than victorious through Him
who loved us. For I am persuaded that
neither death nor life, nor angels nor
rulers, nor things present, nor things
to come, nor powers, nor height, nor
depth, nor any other created thing will
have the power to separate us from the
love of God that is in Christ Jesus our
Lord! ~ Romans 8:35–39

Your Protector Never Sleeps

I lift my eyes toward the mountains.
Where will my help come from? My
help comes from the LORD, the Maker
of heaven and earth. He will not allow
your foot to slip; your Protector will not

slumber. Indeed, the Protector of Israel does not slumber or sleep.

The LORD protects you; the LORD is a shelter right by your side. The sun will not strike you by day, or the moon by night. The LORD will protect you from all harm; He will protect your life. The LORD will protect your coming and going both now and forever. ~ Psalm 121:1–8

Quotes and Sayings

God is always near you and with you; leave Him not alone. ~ Brother Lawrence

God is not far away from us. Rather he awaits us every instant in our action, in the work of the moment. There is a sense in which he is at the tip of my pen, my spake, my brush, my needle. ~ Pierre Teilhard de Chardin

When Jesus is present, all is well, and nothing seems difficult. ~ Thomas à Kempis

The Will of God will never take you where the grace of God cannot keep you. ~ Author Unknown

You are to think of yourself as only existing in this world to do God's will. To think that you are your own is as absurd as to think you are self-created. It is an obvious first principle that you belong completely to God. ~ William Law

Yesterday is history. Tomorrow is a mystery. And today? Today is a gift. That's why we call it the present. ~ Babatunde Olatunji

In God, time and eternity are one and the same thing. ~ Henry Suso

Place a high value upon your time, be more careful of not losing it than you would be of losing your money. Do not let worthless recreations, idle talk, unprofitable company, or sleep rob you of your precious time. Be more careful to escape that person, action or course of life that would rob you of your time than you would be to escape thieves and robbers. ~ Richard Baxter

Promise and Prayer

Dear Lord, help me to be more aware of how I spend my time. Bless me with the presence of mind to live each moment trusting and believing in Your grace and mercy, and doing all I can to live in ways that would please You. Forgive me for the things I did not do well yesterday, and lead me today and ever forward to brighter and more fulfilling tomorrows. Amen.

You and God and the Future

The next moment is as much beyond our grasp, and as much in God's care, as that a hundred years away. Care for the next minute is just as foolish as care for a day in the next thousand years. In neither can we do anything, in both God is doing everything. ~ C. S. Lewis

As a daughter of a heavenly and loving Father, you always have choices about how to live this life. You can start each day opening the baggage from yesterday, reprimanding yourself for the things you did or didn't do, the things you regret or the things you hoped would happen, but did not. You can also start the day without that baggage, leaving yesterday behind and opening your heart and mind to God's leading for today by offering Him your heartfelt prayer.

When you start the day with God, allowing Him to be your first thought before you even let your toes touch the floor, you'll discover that more often than not, you have an incredible day. You are not in control of very much in this life, for even your children are on loan from His grace and merciful throne, but you are in control of how you think and how you handle each day. Handle it with prayer and God will be there with you every step of the way.

The Time Is Near

Look! I am coming quickly, and My reward is with Me to repay each person according to what he has done. I am the Alpha and the Omega, the First and the Last, the Beginning and the End. ~ Revelation 22:12–13

God Is Faithful

Give thanks to the LORD, for He is good; His faithful love endures forever. ~ Psalm 118:1

Be Happy Today

This is the day the LORD has made; let us rejoice and be glad in it. ~ Psalm 118:24

Look to Today

Don't boast about tomorrow, for you don't know what a day might bring. ~ Proverbs 27:1

The Mystery of Time

There is an occasion for everything, and a time for every activity under heaven:

a time to give birth and a time to die; a
time to plant and a time to uproot; a time
to kill and a time to heal; a time to tear
down and a time to build; a time to weep
and a time to laugh; a time to mourn and
a time to dance; a time to throw stones
and a time to gather stones; a time to
embrace and a time to avoid embracing; a
time to search and a time to count as lost;
a time to keep and a time to throw away;
a time to tear and a time to sew; a time
to be silent and a time to speak; a time
to love and a time to hate; a time for war
and a time for peace. ~ Ecclesiastes 3:1–8

God's Plan

As I have purposed, so it will be; as I have
planned it, so it will happen. ~ Isaiah 14:24

Seek God Today and Don't Worry About Tomorrow

But seek first the kingdom of God and
His righteousness, and all these things
will be provided for you. Therefore
don't worry about tomorrow, because
tomorrow will worry about itself. Each
day has enough trouble of its own.
~ Matthew 6:33–34

God Created Time

> For in Your sight a thousand years are like yesterday that passes by, like a few hours of the night. ~ Psalm 90:4

Quotes and Sayings

If God could not be found on this side of the sea we would indeed journey across. Since, however, God is near to everyone who calls on him, we are under no obligation to cross the sea. The kingdom of heaven can be reached from every land. ~ Samhthann

We block Christ's advance in our lives by failure of expectation. Of course this is just one form of lack of faith. But it is so purely negative that it escapes detection. ~ William Temple

The great thing is to be found at one's post as a child of God, living each day as though it were our last, but planning as though our world might last a hundred years. ~ C. S. Lewis

One must know oneself. If this does not serve to discover truth, it at least serves as a rule of life and there is nothing better. ~ Blaise Pascal

Never be afraid to trust an unknown future to a known God. ~ Corrie Ten Boom

Practice hope. As hopefulness becomes a habit, you can achieve a permanently happy spirit. ~ Norman Vincent Peale

Grant me the serenity to accept the things I cannot change; the courage to change the things I can and the wisdom to know the difference. ~ Reinhold Niebhur

The greatest friend of truth is Time, her greatest enemy is Prejudice, and her constant companion is Humility. ~ Charles C. Colton

Promise and Prayer

Lord, even though I do not know what the future might hold for me, I trust in You because I know You hold the future. Please grant me wisdom in the choices I make, guiding my heart and mind in every conversation and every opportunity that comes my way. Remind me that all good things come from Your hand and help me to live my life in ways that honor You and bring praise to Your name. Amen.